DOING *MARRIAGE* *G*OD'S WAY

THE PRACTICES

COUPLE'S DISCUSSION AND ACTIVITY GUIDE

JIMMY EVANS

DOING *MARRIAGE* *G*OD'S WAY

THE PRACTICES

COUPLE'S DISCUSSION AND ACTIVITY GUIDE

JIMMY EVANS

XO
PUBLISHING

XO
PUBLISHING

Doing Marriage God's Way: The Practices: Couple's Discussion and Activity Guide
Copyright © 2025 by Jimmy Evans

ISBN: 978-1-960870-69-8 eBook
ISBN: 978-1-960870-70-4 Paperback

XO Publishing is a leading creator of relationship-based resources. We focus primarily on marriage-related content for churches, small group curriculum, and people looking for timeless truths about relationships and overall marital health. For more information on other resources from XO Publishing, visit XOPublishing.com.

XO Marriage
1021 Grace Lane
Southlake, TX 76092

While the authors make every effort to provide accurate URLs at the time of printing for external or third-party internet websites, neither they nor the publisher assume any responsibility for changes or errors made after publication.

Printed in the United States of America

25 26 27 28—5 4 3 2 1

Table of Contents

Introduction

Welcome to Your Next Level!

If you've completed *Doing Marriage God's Way: The Foundations*, you understand the biblical laws that make marriage work. But understanding principles and living them out daily are two different things. This is what this course is all about—taking God's design and putting it into practice in your everyday life.

WHAT YOU'LL NEED:

- ✓ This guide (just one copy!)
- ✓ Video access
- ✓ 6 sessions, which are usually one week apart, with one dedicated evening for each session (90 minutes)
- ✓ A comfortable, private space for just the two of you
- ✓ Honesty and commitment
- ✓ Optional: A separate notebook for each of you for additional notes

HOW THIS WORKS:

Each week follows this flow:

1. **Prepare**—Set the scene for quality time (5 min)
2. **Watch**—Video teaching together (12-15 min)
3. **Discuss**—Guided conversation (30-40 min)
4. **Apply**—Create your action plan (15-20 min)
5. **Commit**—Agree on weekly practices (5 min)
6. **Pray**—Close in prayer together (5 min)

GROUND RULES:

- Phones off, TV off, distractions eliminated.
- Speak *for* yourself, not *about* your spouse.
- Listen to understand, not to fix or defend.
- Both of you get equal airtime.
- Extend grace—you're both learning.
- Remember: *you're on the same team.*

YOUR WEEKLY TIME:

Day: _____ Time: _____ Location: _____

SESSION 1

How to Understand and Meet Your Wife's Needs

PREPARE (5 MINUTES)

Environment:

- Choose your spot (couch, porch, dining table).
- Eliminate distractions (phones put away).
- Get comfortable.
- Light a candle if you'd like.

Connection Moment:

Before you start, share one way you served each other this past week.

WATCH TOGETHER (15 MINUTES)

As you watch, one person can jot notes here or you can just listen together.

Key Concepts to Listen For:

- The four basic needs that women have
- Why spouses are different than each other
- The servant heart principle
- "Are you okay?" question
- Security as the mega need

DISCUSS (35 MINUTES)

Round 1: The Four Needs Assessment (15 minutes)

Jimmy Evans mentioned the four basic needs that women have: **Security, Non-sexual Affection, Open and Honest Communication, Leadership.**

For the Wife:

Rate how well these needs are being met (1–10):

- Security (feeling sacrificially served and put first): ____/10
- Non-sexual affection (tender touch without sexual agenda): ____/10
- Open and honest communication (detailed conversations): ____/10
- Leadership (loving initiative in home, finances, spirituality): ____/10

For the Husband:

Ask your wife which need she would most like you to focus on this week.

Take turns sharing (5 minutes each, then discuss together):

- Which need feels most important to you right now?
- Which need has been hardest for you to communicate about?

Round 2: The Servant Heart Check (10 minutes)

Discuss together:

- Husband: On a scale of 1–10, how well do I communicate "I'm not okay until you're okay"?
- When have I been defensive instead of serving when you've expressed a need?
- What would change if I truly adopted the mindset "I'm here to serve you"?

Round 3: "Are You Okay?" Practice (10 minutes)

Husband asks:

"Are you okay? Is there anything I'm not doing? Any need I'm not meeting that you wish I would?"

Wife answers honestly:

Husband just listens—no defending, no explaining.

Write down what you heard:

What my wife said she needs: _____

_____

Activity: The Daily Hour Commitment

When and where will you have one hour together daily with no distractions?

Time: _____ Place: _____

Phones will be: _____

What will you do during this time? _____

APPLY (15 MINUTES)

This Week's Husband Action Plan:

Choose one specific action for each need area:

1. **Security:** I will show you come first by: _____
2. **Non-sexual Affection:** I will be tender with you by: _____
3. **Communication:** I will talk with you by: _____
4. **Leadership:** I will lovingly initiate by: _____

Our Communication Commitment:

When will you ask, "Are you okay?" daily? Time: _____
Place: _____

THIS WEEK'S COMMITMENTS

Read aloud together and both say "I commit":

- ☐ **Husband:** I will implement all four actions on my list above.
- ☐ **Wife:** I will clearly communicate my needs without defensiveness.
- ☐ We will protect our daily hour together—no phones, no distractions.
- ☐ We will practice the "Are you okay?" conversation every day.
- ☐ Mid-week check: "How am I doing at meeting your needs?"

PRAY TOGETHER (5 MINUTES)

Prayer Framework:

Husband prays:

- Thank God for your wife.
- Ask for a servant's heart.
- Confess where you've been selfish or defensive.
- Ask God to help you meet her needs.

Wife prays:

- Thank God for your husband's willingness to serve.
- Ask for grace to communicate needs clearly.
- Pray for patience as he learns.

Together:

Hold hands, look into each other's eyes, say "I love you," and then pray the following:

- **Pray for your marriage:** "God, thank You for designing marriage as a reflection of Your love. Help us build our relationship on You every day and keep choosing one another with grace and commitment."

- **Pray for your morning times:** "Give us discipline and desire to seek You first each morning."

- **Pray for transformation:** "Shape us into spouses who build each other up and reflect your character."

- **Pray for the coming week:** "Lead us as we put these practices into action. Remind us that every small act of love strengthens our marriage and honors You."

- **Close with commitment:** Each person says, "I choose to seek Jesus first." Say "Amen" together.

THIS WEEK'S DATE NIGHT

Date Idea: Go somewhere you can talk—coffee shop, quiet restaurant, or a walk. Focus entirely on conversation.

Date Night Questions:

- "What made you feel most loved when we were dating?"
- "How can I better serve you in our marriage?"
- "What would our marriage look like if I truly put you first every day?"

NOTES

SESSION 2

How to Understand and Meet Your Husband's Needs

PREPARE (5 MINUTES)

Before you start, share: "What did you notice this week when your needs were being met?"

WATCH TOGETHER (15 MINUTES)

Key Concepts to Listen For:

- The four core needs that men have
- Honor as the mega need of men
- The difference between honoring and being a mother
- The power of prayer over confrontation
- "Fighting fire with water"

DISCUSS (35 MINUTES)

Round 1: The Four Needs Assessment (15 minutes)

Jimmy Evans mentioned the four basic needs that men have: **Honor, Sex, Friendship, Domestic Support.**

For the Husband:

Rate how well these needs are being met (1–10):

- Honor (respect, appreciation, being treated well): ___/10
- Sex (physical intimacy and sexual fulfillment): ___/10
- Friendship (being buddies, doing things together): ___/10
- Domestic Support (home being a peaceful, welcoming place): ___/10

For the Wife:

Ask your husband which need he would most like you to focus on this week.

Take turns sharing (5 minutes each, then discuss together):

- Which need feels most important to you right now?
- When do you feel most honored vs. most disrespected?

Round 2: The Honor Check (10 minutes)

Wife reflects:

- On a scale of 1–10, how well do I honor my husband with my words and attitude?
- When do I tend to treat him more like a child than a partner?
- How do I respond when he fails or makes mistakes?

Husband shares:

- What makes you feel most respected and honored?
- What makes you feel criticized or controlled?

Round 3: The Cork Principle (10 minutes)

Discuss the "cork principle" Pastor Jimmy mentioned:

- **Wife:** In what areas do I try to "talk to the cork" instead of "filling the vessel with honor"?
- **Husband:** How do you respond when you feel honored vs. when you feel criticized?
- What would change if honor became the primary way we addressed issues?

Activity: Prayer vs. Confrontation

Wife commits:

Instead of criticizing or nagging about _____, I will:

1. Speak to my husband respectfully about it once.
2. Pray about it daily.
3. Trust God to change his heart.

APPLY (15 MINUTES)

This Week's Wife Action Plan:

Choose one specific action for each need area:

1. **Honor:** I will show respect by: _____.
2. **Sex:** I will be more available/initiating by: _____.
3. **Friendship:** I will be your buddy by: _____.
4. **Domestic Support:** I will make our home welcoming by: _____.

Our Honor Agreement:

Wife commits to:

- Speaking to my husband the way I would speak to Jesus
- Praying for my husband daily instead of criticizing
- Honoring him even when he doesn't deserve it

Husband commits to:

- Rising to the level of honor my wife gives me
- Being worthy of respect through my actions
- Not taking advantage of my wife's honoring attitude

THIS WEEK'S COMMITMENTS

Read aloud together and both say "I commit":

- ☐ **Wife:** I will implement all four actions on my list above.
- ☐ **Husband:** I will respond positively to honor and work to deserve it.
- ☐ We will continue our daily hour together.
- ☐ Wife will pray for husband daily instead of criticizing.
- ☐ Mid-week check: "Do you feel honored and respected this week?"

PRAY TOGETHER (5 MINUTES)

Prayer Framework:

Wife prays:

- Thank God for your husband.
- Ask for wisdom to honor him properly.
- Confess where you've been disrespectful or controlling.
- Pray for God to work in his heart.

Husband prays:

- Thank God for your wife's respect.
- Ask God to help you be worthy of honor.
- Pray for wisdom to meet her needs in return.

THIS WEEK'S DATE NIGHT

Date Idea: Do something your husband enjoys—watch a game together, go to his favorite restaurant, try his hobby.

Date Night Activity:

- Focus on being his friend and companion.
- Ask him about his interests, his day, his dreams.
- Practice honoring him through your attention and words.

NOTES

_____

_____

_____

_____

_____

_____

_____

_____

_____

_____

_____

_____

_____

_____

_____

_____

_____

SESSION 3

Communication: Building Your Bridge

PREPARE (5 MINUTES)

Before you start, share: "What's one way you felt honored/served this week that meant a lot?"

WATCH TOGETHER (15 MINUTES)

Key Concepts to Listen For:

- Speaking truth in love
- The five keys to communication
- Difference between complaining and criticizing
- The importance of daily face-to-face time
- Caring, listening, praising, confronting, openness

DISCUSS (35 MINUTES)

Round 1: Communication Assessment (15 minutes)

Rate your current communication (1–10):

Caring:

- We make eye contact when talking: _____/10
- We eliminate distractions during important conversations: _____/10
- We both feel heard and valued: _____/10

Listening:

- I listen to understand, not just to respond: _____/10
- I listen for emotions, not just words: _____/10
- My spouse feels truly heard by me: _____/10

Praising:

- I regularly praise my spouse: _____/10
- I focus on positives more than negatives: _____/10
- I speak life, not death, over my spouse: _____/10

Share your numbers with each other and discuss: What do these numbers reveal?

Round 2: Complaint vs. Criticism Practice (10 minutes)

Pastor Jimmy's example:

- **Criticism:** "You always do this because you're just like your mother and you're trying to get back at me..."
- **Complaint:** "When you said that yesterday, I have no idea what you meant. Can I tell you how it made me feel?"

Practice round:

Think of something that bothered you recently. Each person practice stating it as a complaint, not criticism:

Criticism format: "You always..." "You never..." "You did this because..."

Complaint format: "When _____ happened, I felt _____. Can we talk about it?"

Round 3: Daily Communication Commitment (10 minutes)

Our Daily Hour:

- When: _____
- Where: _____
- No phones: ☐
- No TV: ☐
- No kids interrupting: ☐
- Face-to-face: ☐

What we'll do during this time:

- Check in about our day
- Share feelings and emotions
- Ask "Are you okay?"
- Praise each other
- Address any concerns lovingly

APPLY (15 MINUTES)

Activity: The Five Keys Practice

This week, we commit to:

1. **Caring:** We will make eye contact and eliminate distractions during conversations.
2. **Listening:** We will listen for heart, not just words.
3. **Praising:** We will each give three specific praises daily.
4. **Confronting:** We will complain, not criticize, when we have concerns.
5. **Openness:** We will not be defensive when our spouse shares concerns.

Our Praise Commitment

Each day this week, we will share:

- One thing we appreciate about each other.
- One thing we admire about each other.
- One way we saw God working through each other.

Our Confrontation Agreement

When we need to address something difficult:

- We will start with "I love you and I'm committed to our marriage."
- We will use "I feel" statements, not "You always" statements.
- We will listen without defending.
- We will work toward resolution, not just venting.

THIS WEEK'S COMMITMENTS

Read aloud together and both say "I commit":

- ☐ We will protect our daily communication hour.
- ☐ We will practice the five keys to communication.
- ☐ We will praise each other three times daily.
- ☐ We will complain, not criticize, when we have concerns.
- ☐ We will practice openness without defensiveness.

PRAY TOGETHER (5 MINUTES)

Prayer Framework:

- ◆ Thank God for the gift of communication.
- ◆ Confess where you've hurt each other with words.
- ◆ Ask for wisdom to speak truth in love.
- ◆ Pray for open, honest hearts toward each other.

THIS WEEK'S DATE NIGHT

Date Idea: Have an "unplugged" evening—no phones, no TV. Cook together, play a board game, or just talk.

Date Night Activity:

Practice the five keys to communication. Share childhood memories, dreams for the future, or just enjoy talking without any agenda except connection.

NOTES

_____

_____

_____

_____

_____

_____

_____

_____

_____

_____

_____

_____

_____

_____

_____

_____

_____

SESSION 4

Money: Seven Principles for Financial Success

PREPARE (5 MINUTES)

Before you start, share: "What's the best conversation we've had this week?"

WATCH TOGETHER (15 MINUTES)

Key Concepts to Listen For:

- Four money languages (Driver, Analytic, Amiable, Expressive)
- Respect for different money perspectives
- Partnership in financial decisions
- The principle of giving first
- Contentment vs. debt

DISCUSS (35 MINUTES)

Round 1: Money Language Assessment (15 minutes)

Identify your money language:

Driver (Money = Success)

- I see money as a way to achieve and accomplish.
- I like to make financial decisions quickly.
- I'm motivated by financial goals and winning.

Analytic (Money = Security)

- ◆ I see money as protection against uncertainty.
- ◆ I prefer to save and be conservative.
- ◆ I want to avoid financial risk.

Amiable (Money = Love)

- ◆ I see money as a way to express care and love.
- ◆ I enjoy giving gifts and experiences.
- ◆ I like to use money to bless others.

Expressive (Money = Acceptance)

- ◆ I see money as a way to fit in and be accepted.
- ◆ I enjoy nice things and experiences.
- ◆ I like money for what it can do socially.

Each person circle your primary money language above.

Now discuss:

- ◆ How are our money languages different?
- ◆ Where have we judged each other's approach to money?
- ◆ How can our different approaches actually help us make better decisions together?

Round 2: Financial Respect and Partnership (10 minutes)

Honest assessment:

- ◆ Have we called each other names about money? (spendthrift, tightwad, materialistic, cheap)
- ◆ Do we make financial decisions together or independently?
- ◆ Do we respect each other's money perspective or try to change it?

Pastor Jimmy's Disneyland example:

He wanted to go, Karen wanted to save first. They did both—expressed love through the trip *and* maintained security by saving first.

How can we combine our money languages for better decisions?

Round 3: Giving and Contentment (10 minutes)

Our current giving:

- Do we give to our local church? Yes / No
- Do we tithe (10%)? Yes / No
- Do we give offerings beyond the tithe? Yes / No

Our current debt situation:

- Do we live below, at, or above our means? Yes / No
- Do we have credit card debt? Yes / No
- Do we feel financial pressure regularly? Yes / No

Discuss Pastor Jimmy's testimony:

When Karen started giving $40 (which they didn't have), it was the first time they weren't overdrawn. How might God want to bless our obedience in giving?

APPLY (15 MINUTES)

Activity: Our Financial Agreement

We commit to:

1. **Respect:** We will stop judging each other's money language and appreciate our differences.
2. **Partnership:** We will make all financial decisions together and won't spend over $_____ without agreement.
3. **Giving:** We will give _____% to our local church starting this week.
4. **Contentment:** We will wait and save for purchases over $_____ instead of going into debt.
5. **Communication:** We will have a monthly money meeting to review our budget and goals.

Our Money Languages Working Together:

How _____ (husband's money language) can help us: _____.

How _____ (wife's money language) can help us: _____.

Our Monthly Budget Meeting:

When: _____ Where: _____

What we'll review:

- Income and expenses
- Giving
- Savings goals
- Any purchases we want to make
- How we're feeling about our finances

THIS WEEK'S COMMITMENTS

Read aloud together and both say "I commit":

- ☐ We will respect each other's money language and stop using negative labels.
- ☐ We will make all financial decisions together as partners.
- ☐ We will start/increase our giving to our local church.
- ☐ We will create a plan to get out of debt if we have any.
- ☐ We will schedule our monthly budget meeting.

PRAY TOGETHER (5 MINUTES)

Prayer Framework:

- Thank God for His provision in your lives.
- Confess any wrong attitudes about money.
- Ask God to bless your giving and your partnership.
- Pray for wisdom in financial decisions.

THIS WEEK'S DATE NIGHT

Date Idea: Have a "budget date"—make it fun! Get coffee or dessert and work on your budget together.

Date Night Activity:

- Create your first budget together respecting both money languages.
- Discuss your financial dreams and goals.
- Plan your first act of giving or increased giving.

NOTES

SESSION 5

Practicing Safe Technology

PREPARE (5 MINUTES)

Before you start, share: "How did our financial conversation change things this week?"

WATCH TOGETHER (15 MINUTES)

Key Concepts to Listen For:

- Statistics about technology's impact on marriage
- Three rules of intimacy
- Privacy, living human contact, and boundaries
- Technology as servant vs. master
- The need for device-free times and zones

DISCUSS (35 MINUTES)

Round 1: Technology Reality Check (15 minutes)

Honest Assessment

Check your phone settings for screen time this week:

- Hours per day on phone: Husband _____ Wife _____
- Most used apps: _____
- Times checked per day: _____

Rate these statements (1–10, 10 being "always true"):

- I can have a conversation without checking my phone: ____/10
- My spouse gets my full attention when they're talking: ____/10
- We have phone-free time together daily: ____/10
- Technology never comes between us during intimate moments: ____/10
- I can turn off my phone without anxiety: ____/10

Pastor Jimmy's Statistics

- 33% of divorces start as online affairs.
- 1 in 7 married people contemplate divorce due to spouse's social media activity.
- 10% of people check phones during sex.

How do these statistics make you feel about our technology use?

Round 2: The Three Rules of Intimacy (10 minutes)

Rule 1: Intimacy requires privacy

- When do we have true privacy (no devices) together?
- What prevents us from being alone together?

Rule 2: Intimacy requires living human contact

- How much eye contact do we actually make daily?
- When do we touch without devices in our hands?

Rule 3: Intimacy requires boundaries

- What boundaries do we currently have with technology?
- Where do we need better boundaries?

Round 3: Current Problems (10 minutes)

Be honest about these scenarios:

- Do you answer your phone during conversations with your spouse?
- Do you check your phone while your spouse is talking to you?
- Do you use devices in the bedroom?
- Do you have passwords your spouse doesn't know?
- Have you ever had an inappropriate conversation online?

Discuss openly and without defensiveness what needs to change.

APPLY (15 MINUTES)

Activity: Our Technology Boundaries

Our Device-Free Times:

- Daily: From _____ to _____ (minimum 1 hour face-to-face time)
- During meals: Yes / No devices
- In bedroom: Yes / No devices
- During conversations: Yes / No devices

Our Device-Free Zones:

- Bedroom: Yes / No
- Dining room: Yes / No
- Car: Yes / No
- Date nights: Yes / No

Our Accountability Agreement:

- We will share all passwords: Yes / No
- We won't have private conversations with opposite sex: Yes / No
- We will tell each other if technology is bothering us: Yes / No
- We can ask each other to put devices away without offense: Yes / No

Our Daily Phone-Free Hour: When: _____

Where: _____ What we'll do: _____

This Week's Technology Fast:

Choose one:

- One evening completely device-free
- No phones during all meals
- No devices in bedroom for entire week
- One full day without social media

We choose: _____

THIS WEEK'S COMMITMENTS

Read aloud together and both say "I commit":

- ☐ We will implement our device-free times and zones.
- ☐ We will share passwords and be completely transparent.
- ☐ We will prioritize face-to-face time over digital connection.
- ☐ We will complete our technology fast.
- ☐ We will lovingly point out when technology is coming between us.

PRAY TOGETHER (5 MINUTES)

Prayer Framework:

- Thank God for the gift of each other.
- Confess where technology has hurt your relationship.
- Ask for wisdom to use technology as a servant, not master.
- Pray for protection from online temptations.

THIS WEEK'S DATE NIGHT

Date Idea: Have a completely unplugged date—leave phones at home. Go for a walk, have dinner, or just sit and talk.

Date Night Challenge: See how long you can go without missing your devices. Focus entirely on each other and enjoy being fully present.

NOTES

SESSION 6

When You're Building Alone and Moving Forward

PREPARE (5 MINUTES)

Before you start, share: "How did our technology boundaries change our connection this week?"

WATCH TOGETHER (15 MINUTES)

Key Concepts to Listen For:

- First Peter 3 and redemptive love
- Four principles for building alone
- Difference between suffering and abuse
- The power of prayer over confrontation
- Hope for seemingly impossible situations

DISCUSS (35 MINUTES)

Round 1: Honest Assessment (15 minutes)

This session is for when one spouse is more committed than the other. Be completely honest:

- Are we both equally committed to making our marriage work? Yes / No
- Is one of us carrying more of the load in working on our relationship? If yes, who?
- Are there areas where one spouse is destructive or unwilling to change?

If both spouses are equally committed: Use this session to understand how to help other couples who may be struggling.

If one spouse is less committed: Listen with humility and without defensiveness.

Important Distinction—Pastor Jimmy emphasized the difference:

- **Suffering:** Uncomfortable situation, going through difficulty
- **Abuse:** Damage, harm, violence (physical, verbal, emotional)

If there is abuse present, seek help immediately. This session is not for abusive situations.

Round 2: The Four Principles (15 minutes)

For the spouse who is building alone, or both spouses to understand these principles:

1. Submission to God

- "I want my marriage, but I'll do it God's way."
- No threats, no sin, no revenge
- Trusting God to change hearts

2. Willingness to Suffer

- Accepting that change takes time
- Going through difficulty righteously
- Not putting up with abuse, but being patient with process

3. Vision

- Believing God for the marriage He wants you to have
- Reading Ephesians 5 and praying it over your spouse
- Not letting current reality dictate future possibilities

4. Positive Support

- Having mature, godly people pray with you
- Getting help when needed (intervention for serious issues)
- Staying encouraged to do the right thing

Which of these is hardest for you? Why?

Round 3: Redemptive Love in Action (5 minutes)

Pastor Jimmy's example: Karen stopped fighting with words and started serving him with actions and prayer. This broke through when words couldn't.

Practical redemptive love looks like:

- Treating your spouse better than they deserve
- Doing the right thing when they do the wrong thing
- Praying instead of nagging
- Serving instead of demanding

How could redemptive love change your specific situation?

APPLY (15 MINUTES)

Activity: Building Hope and Action

If you're both committed:

Our mutual commitment:

- We both agree we're fully committed to doing whatever it takes to have a great marriage.
- We will encourage each other when one of us is struggling or discouraged.
- We will practice redemptive love even in small conflicts, treating each other better than we deserve.

If one spouse is less committed:

For the committed spouse:

This week I will practice redemptive love by:

1. _____
2. _____
3. _____

Instead of trying to change my spouse through words/arguments, I will:

- Pray for them daily.
- Treat them better than they deserve.
- Trust God to work in their heart.

People who will pray with me:

1. _____
2. _____

For the less committed spouse:

If you're willing: What would it look like for you to become more committed to working on your marriage?

If you're not ready: That's honest. The committed spouse will practice redemptive love regardless of your response.

THIS WEEK'S COMMITMENTS

If both are committed, read aloud together and both say "I commit":

- ☐ We will both work equally hard on our marriage.
- ☐ We will practice redemptive love toward each other.
- ☐ We will pray for each other daily.
- ☐ We will encourage each other's growth.

If one is building alone: Committed spouse: "I commit to loving you redemptively, praying for you daily, and trusting God with the results."

PRAY TOGETHER (5 MINUTES)

If both are committed:

- Thank God for each other's commitment.
- Ask for strength to practice redemptive love.
- Pray for continued growth in your marriage.

If one is building alone, committed spouse prays aloud:

- Thank God for your spouse.
- Ask God to work in their heart.
- Commit to loving them redemptively.
- Ask for strength and patience.

THIS WEEK'S DATE NIGHT

If both are committed: Celebrate your mutual commitment. Go somewhere special and share your dreams for your marriage.

If one is building alone: The committed spouse can still initiate a kind gesture—not to manipulate, but to show love. Maybe a simple coffee together or a walk.

NOTES

Course Completion

Living Out the Practices

Celebrate!

You've invested in the practical application of God's design for marriage. Well done!

Reflection Questions:

Discuss together:

- What practice has made the biggest difference in our marriage?
- Which area do we still need to work on most?
- How are we different now compared to when we started?

THE SIX PRACTICES REVIEW

Together, rate yourselves on each practice (1–10):

1. **Understanding and Meeting Wife's Needs**
   Our rating: ____/10
   What we're doing well: _____
   What needs work: _____

2. **Understanding and Meeting Husband's Needs**
   Our rating: ____/10
   What we're doing well: _____
   What needs work: _____

3. **Communication**
   Our rating: ____/10
   What we're doing well: _____
   What needs work: _____

4. Financial Partnership
Our rating: _____/10
What we're doing well: _____
What needs work: _____

5. Technology Boundaries
Our rating: _____/10
What we're doing well: _____
What needs work: _____

6. Building Together (or Redemptive Love)
Our rating: _____/10
What we're doing well: _____
What needs work: _____

YOUR 90-DAY ACTION PLAN

Our Priority Practice:

Based on your ratings, which practice needs the most attention in the next 90 days?

We choose: _____

Our Specific Action Plan:

Daily, we will:

_____

Weekly, we will:

_____

Monthly, we will:

_____

Our Weekly Marriage Check-In:

Day: _____ Time: _____ Place: _____

What we'll do during this time:

- Review our progress on our priority practice.
- Ask "Are you okay?"
- Rate our practices (1-10).
- Pray together.
- Adjust as needed.

YOUR MARRIAGE PRACTICE COVENANT

Read this out loud together, then sign below:

"We covenant before God to live out these biblical practices daily.

We will:

- Serve each other by meeting our specific needs.
- Communicate with truth and love using the five keys.
- Honor our different money languages and make financial decisions together.
- Keep technology as our servant, not our master
- Practice redemptive love, especially when it's difficult.
- Keep learning, growing, and applying what we've learned.

We recognize that marriage requires daily practice, but when we live out these principles consistently, our marriage becomes what God designed it to be."

Signed:

Husband:_____ Date: _____

Wife: _____ Date: _____

WHERE DO WE GO FROM HERE?

Immediate Next Steps:

Check what you'll do:

- ☐ Put our weekly check-in on the calendar for the next 3 months.
- ☐ Schedule our next date night.
- ☐ Continue our daily communication hour.
- ☐ Implement our 90-day action plan.
- ☐ Find another couple to mentor using these practices.
- ☐ Continue in marriage coaching/counseling.
- ☐ Start another marriage study.
- ☐ Join a couples small group.

NON-NEGOTIABLES

Read these aloud together and commit:

We will maintain these practices:

- **Daily:** Personal time with Jesus (individually)
- **Daily:** "Are you okay?" conversation
- **Daily:** One hour face-to-face with no distractions
- **Daily:** Technology boundaries we've established
- **Weekly:** Date night
- **Weekly:** Marriage check-in using material from this course
- **Monthly:** Review our financial partnership
- **Yearly:** Marriage retreat or getaway

A LETTER TO YOUR FUTURE SELVES

Write this together. Open it in one year.

Date: _____

Dear Us in One Year,

Today we finished the "Doing Marriage God's Way: The Practices" course.

Here's what we learned:

_____

_____

_____

Here's what we're committing to:

_____

_____

_____

Here's what we hope is true a year from now:

_____

_____

_____

We love each other. We're practicing God's design together. Our marriage is growing stronger every day.

Signed, _____ and _____

Seal this letter. Put it somewhere safe. Open it one year from today.

FINAL PRAYER TOGETHER

Hold hands. Look at each other. Pray together:

Husband, pray:

- Thank God for your wife.
- Commit to practicing what you've learned.
- Ask for daily strength to serve her well.

Wife, pray:

- Thank God for your husband.
- Commit to practicing what you've learned.
- Ask for daily wisdom to honor him.

Together, pray:

"God, thank You for these six weeks of learning to practice Your design for marriage. Help us live out what we've learned every single day. When we fail, help us practice redemptive love. When we succeed, help us stay humble. Build our house on the Rock. We trust You. In Jesus' name. Amen."

Kiss each other. Celebrate your commitment to practicing God's design for marriage!

Appendix

Quick Reference

WIFE'S FOUR NEEDS:

1. **Security**—Sacrificial service, being put first
2. **Non-sexual Affection**—Tender touch without agenda
3. **Open and Honest Communication**—Detailed conversations
4. **Leadership**—Loving initiative in home, finances, spirituality

HUSBAND'S FOUR NEEDS:

1. **Honor**—Respect, appreciation, being treated well
2. **Sex**—Physical intimacy and sexual fulfillment
3. **Friendship**—Being buddies, doing things together
4. **Domestic Support**—Home being peaceful and welcoming

FIVE KEYS TO COMMUNICATION:

1. **Caring**—Eye contact, undistracted attention
2. **Listening**—Hearing heart, not just words
3. **Praising**—Speaking life, not death
4. **Confronting**—Complaining, not criticizing
5. **Openness**—Non-defensive responses

FOUR MONEY LANGUAGES:

1. **Driver**—Money = Success
2. **Analytic**—Money = Security
3. **Amiable**—Money = Love
4. **Expressive**—Money = Acceptance

TECHNOLOGY BOUNDARIES:

- Intimacy requires privacy, human contact, and boundaries
- Daily device-free time together
- Technology is servant, not master
- Complete transparency with devices

FOUR PRINCIPLES FOR BUILDING ALONE:

1. Submission to God
2. Willingness to Suffer (not abuse)
3. Vision for God's Best
4. Positive Support

EMERGENCY RESET PHRASES:

- "Are you okay?"
- "I'm here to serve you."
- "How can I meet your needs better?"
- "I'm sorry. I was wrong. Will you forgive me?"
- "We're on the same team."

Final Word

Marriage is built through daily practices, not just understanding principles.

These six practices are the bridge between knowing God's design and living it out.

Practice them daily. When you fail, practice redemptive love. When you succeed, stay humble.

Remember: "Unless the Lord builds the house, the builders labor in vain." (Psalm 127:1)

Let God build your house through these daily practices.

Therefore encourage one another and build each other up, just as in fact you are doing.

—1 Thessalonians 5:11